INSIDE...

Words in bold are in the glossary.

Werewolves all around!

Many legends tell of werewolves that look like ordinary people by day. It is only at night that their true form is revealed. Their bodies are gripped with the werewolf **curse** as they change into bloodthirsty killers.

Worldwide threat

Today, werewolves have spread around the world. Almost anywhere you go, you will hear stories of **shape-shifting** humans who become wolf-like when the moon is full. Not all werewolves are evil killers. Some do no harm. But their bloodthirsty **kindred** more than make up for these peaceable werewolves.

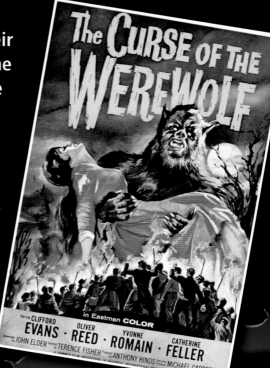

▼ Werewolves have featured in many films over the years.

Werewolf Hunter's Kit

No sensible werewolf hunter would be without the following weapons:

• Silver weapons kill werewolves. Silver swords and bullets are particularly good.

———— Silver weapons and bullets

▲ *This unlucky traveller has met up with a werewolf. Now, he will never reach home.*

The werewolf hunters

All that stands between ferocious killer werewolves and normal people is a select band of werewolf hunters. They know how werewolves act, the danger signs that one is around, and the best ways to destroy a werewolf. This guide contains their secrets. Reading it is your first step on the road to becoming a werewolf hunter.

- Wolfbane, a plant that grows around the world. It is poisonous to humans, as well as werewolves.

- Plants, such as rye and mistletoe, and berries from the mountain ash tree are also said to safeguard you against werewolf attack.

Mistletoe

Mountain ash berries

Wolfbane

5

Werewolf characteristics

Werewolves appear in different forms. A good werewolf hunter needs to be able to recognise all of them.

Some werewolves look like wolves once they have been **transformed**. Other werewolves look more like a cross between a wolf and a human. Many stories suggest that the change from human to werewolf is triggered by the full moon.

Recognising werewolves

These are some of the clues that someone may be a werewolf:

• Eyebrows that meet in the middle.

• Red hair, or hairs on the palms of the hands.

• If the skin is cut open, there will be fur underneath it.

• Loves raw or slightly cooked meat.

• Born on Christmas Day.

▼ *A night lit by a full moon. This is the time of each month when you are most likely to meet a werewolf.*

▼ *This werewolf is a terrifying cross between a wolf and a human.*

Key werewolf characteristics

Whatever form they take, all werewolves have some things in common:

- They are unbelievably strong.
- They can run long distances at speed, and climb high walls with ease.
- In wolf form, they have no tail, and keep their human eyes and voice.

Some werewolves are **immune** to ordinary weapons (though never to silver bullets), and can only be killed when in human form.

The werewolf's bite

The usual way for people to become a werewolf is to be bitten by one. Most people who get bitten by a werewolf die, of course. But if they survive, they will become a werewolf themselves.

HOW WEREWOLVES ARE MADE

The usual way for people to become a werewolf is being bitten by one. But there are plenty of other ways to become a werewolf:

- Being cursed by a witch or magician.
- Being smeared with a special potion.
- Falling asleep outside with a full moon on your face on a Wednesday or a Friday.

The legend of Sigmund and Sinfjotli

The legend of Sigmund and Sinfjotli comes from the frozen lands of the North.

Werewolf Fact File

Name: Varulfur
Location: Iceland
Age: at least 500 years

One day, Sigmund and Sinfjotli are out hunting. They find a cabin with two men asleep inside. Next to the sleepers lie two large wolf skins. The skins look so fine and warm that Sigmund and Sinfjotli creep forwards, and try them on. Too late, they realise their mistake! The skins are cursed. They transform the wearer into a wolf.

A promise

The curse of the skins lasts for nine days. Until then, Sigmund and Sinfjotli must survive as wolves. They decide to separate, but each promises to come if the other is attacked or hunted by men.

▼ Many werewolf stories come from the icy lands of Iceland and Scandinavia.

▲ *Sigmund and Sinfjotli are transformed by the cursed skins into howling wolves.*

Hunted

Sigmund and Sinfjotli's promise is soon put to the test. When a group of hunters chase after Sigmund, he howls out to his friend Sinfjotli for help. Sinfjotli races to his aid, and together they kill every hunter. But then more hunters appear. Sinfjotli is pursued by 11 men, but he doesn't call his friend for help. Instead, he kills all of the hunters by himself.

Werewolf fight!

When Sigmund discovers what has happened, he asks why Sinfjotli did not call for help. Sinfjotli replies arrogantly that – unlike Sigmund – he did not need any help. Furious, Sigmund attacks, biting Sinfjotli in the throat. Then, **wracked** with guilt, he carries Sinfjotli back to the cabin in the woods. As he arrives, a raven brings him a magical plant, which heals Sinfjotli's wounds.

By now, the nine days are up, and the werewolf curse has lifted. Instead of leaving the skins for others to find, Sigmund and Sinfjotli burn them – making sure that there are two fewer werewolves than before.

9

Pricolici of Romania

The mountains of Romania can be dangerous territory. Many strange and deadly creatures survive there, such as the pricolici. Pricolici are werewolves, but have many vampire **traits**.

Pricolici behaviour

Pricolici are the remains of humans who are dead and buried, but rise up from their graves at night. They take the shape of wolves. Pricolici attack the living silently and with terrible violence, drinking their blood and eating their flesh.

▼ *If you visit the lonely, inhospitable valleys of Central Europe, beware – there may be pricolici on the prowl here.*

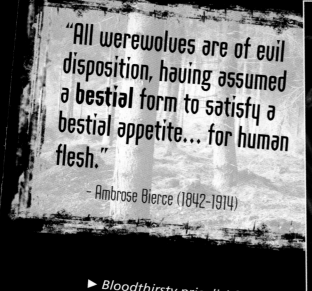

> "All werewolves are of evil disposition, having assumed a **bestial** form to satisfy a bestial appetite... for human flesh."
>
> – Ambrose Bierce (1842–1914)

► Bloodthirsty pricolici feature in many Romanian horror films.

Discovering pricolici

It is said that if the grave of a pricolici is dug up, it will be found lying face down with its rear in the air, and will have blood on its lips. This blood, if given to any of the pricolici's victims who are still alive, will make them well again, and will take away the werewolf curse.

▼ An old graveyard in Romania. Could one of these headstones have a pricolici sheltering beneath it?

Fighting and destroying

Because they have so much in common with vampires, pricolici can be fought and destroyed in the same ways:

• A stake through the heart.
• A silver bullet.
• Cutting off their head and stuffing their mouth with garlic.

Some stories also claim that if pricolici are caught out of their grave during daylight, they will be destroyed.

11

Vilkacis of Latvia and Lithuania

In northern Europe, on the shores of the cold Baltic Sea, are the lands of Latvia and Lithuania. These bleak, windswept countries are home to the vilkacis, which are among Europe's oldest werewolves.

Werewolf Fact File

Name: Vilkacis (male), vilkatas (female)
Location: Latvia and Lithuania
Age: several hundred years

What is a vilkacis?

Most people say that vilkacis are humans who turn into wolves. A few people say that they are people who can transport their souls into the body of a wolf. However the transformation happens, most stories agree that the vilkacis is more likely to attack animals such as cattle or sheep than humans.

◀ *Could this snarling wolf in fact be a vilkacis?*

Becoming a vilkacis

Being bitten by a vilkacis is a sure way to become one yourself, but it's not the only one. There are at least two other ways in which people can become a vilkacis:

- When the moon is full, sleep under a tree whose tip has curled down to touch the soil.
- Wrap yourself in a wolf's skin and say an **incantation.**

Vilkacis are unusual among werewolves because they have no special powers or protection. They can be shot or got rid of in the same way as ordinary wolves.

TRAPPED AS A WOLF

Some stories say that when women become vilkatas they must leave their clothes hidden where no one can find them. If the clothes are touched while the woman is in wolf form, she will not be able to become human again. Instead, she is cursed to stay a wolf for nine years.

▼ *A vilkacis in the midst of transformation.*

13

The Jura werewolves

This story is the tragic case of the Gandillon family. They lived over 400 years ago in the mountainous Jura region, on the border between France and Switzerland. Almost the entire family became infected with the werewolf curse – with terrible **consequences**.

Werewolf Fact File

Name: Gandillon family
Location: Jura Mountains, France
Date: 1598

▼ The thick forests and steep valleys of the Jura region are an ideal place for werewolves to hunt.

An attack

One day, two small children were attacked by a wolf in a forest in Jura. One of the children cut the wolf with a knife, and it fled. A group of hunters was soon on the wolf's trail – but when they found it, they got a terrible surprise.

The first werewolf

What the hunters found was not a wolf, but a young woman called Pernette Gandillon. She was covered in blood, and cut in the same place as the wolf had been. Soon afterwards, a crowd of angry villagers **lynched** Pernette, convinced that she was a werewolf.

▲ The Gandillons were able to transform themselves into wolves at will, and struck fear into local families with their brutal attacks.

More Gandillon werewolves

Soon after Pernette's death, her sister, brother and nephew were arrested. The sister quickly admitted that she was a witch. The two men began to behave very strangely. They started to run about their prison cell on all fours, snarling and barking at people. They confessed to being Devil-worshipping werewolves.

Since Devil worship, being a werewolf and witchcraft were all punishable by death, there could only be one outcome. All three surviving Gandillons were burned alive.

WEREWOLF TRANSFORMATION

The Gandillons claimed to become werewolves using a special potion they had got from the Devil. They rubbed it on their skin to become wolves. To return to human form, they rolled in damp grass until the potion had been removed.

The skinwalkers of North America

Imagine yourself out in the wilds of North America. Suddenly, you're aware of a wolf, slipping along beside you. But there's something strange about it. Is it a wolf – or could it be a skinwalker?

Werewolf Fact File

Name: Skinwalkers
Location: North America
Age: Several hundred years

◄ Skinwalkers are so-called because they steal the 'skin' of their victim. This skinwalker has stolen a human skin.

Skinwalker characteristics

Skinwalkers are humans who can shape-shift into animal form, usually a coyote or wolf. They can read human minds and copy human voices.

Detection and destruction

In its human form, it is almost impossible to spot a skinwalker. The only way is to track the creature in its animal form back to its home. Skinwalkers, like other werewolves, will have the same injuries as the animal version – this can be a way of picking them out.

In animal form, it is easy to spot a skinwalker. They cannot walk in the same way as a real animal, as they are less agile. The Navajo Native Americans say that you can destroy a skinwalker if you find out its human identity. Say the skinwalker's human name, then shout: 'You are a skinwalker!' Within three days it will be dead.

▶ The skinwalker's favourite animal form is the coyote.

PROTECTION AGAINST SKINWALKERS

Protect yourself against attack by covering your body with one of the following:
• The ash of a cedar tree
• The juice of juniper berries
• Corn pollen (but it's very tricky to collect!)

Rougarou of Louisiana

Werewolf Fact File

Name: Rougarou
Location: southern Louisiana, USA
Age: several hundred years

In southern Louisiana, USA, lie the 'Bottoms'. These misty, damp swamps are mysterious and eerie places. Poisonous snakes and alligators are not the only dangers here – this is where rougarou hunt for their victims.

▼ *It is in swampy wetlands like this one that you are most in danger of meeting a rougarou.*

Detection

Rougarou are werewolves with a terrible hunger for human flesh. A rougarou, like so many werewolves, is difficult to tell from a normal person during the day.

One sign can be that someone is always very tired because they have been hunting for victims at night. After dark, rougarou take on their werewolf form. They have a human body, but the head of a wolf.

People become rougarou by being bitten by a rougarou. Once infected, it is impossible to shed the werewolf curse during the first 101 days. On the 102nd day the curse can be passed on by biting someone else.

Killing rougarou

Some stories say that a rougarou can only be killed either by burning or by cutting off its head. In its human form, a rougarou can be killed just like any other person.

▲ If you hear howling in the swamps, and there's a full moon – watch out! There's a rougarou about.

RELIGIOUS ENFORCER

Many stories tell how rougarou seek out bad Catholics as their victims. If you don't stick to the rules of **Lent**, in particular, watch out for rougarou coming out of the swamp to get you!

The Beast of Bray Road

Around the time of the full moon, the residents of the little town of Elkhorn, Wisconsin USA, are careful to lock their doors at night. They stick to brightly lit areas, and stay away from the woods. Why? They don't want to run into the Beast.

Werewolf Fact File

Name: The Beast
Location: Wisconsin and Illinois, USA
Age: first reported 1936

The Beast has appeared many times since it was first spotted in 1936. Most witnesses describe it as a large, wolf-like creature that goes around on its hind legs. It is 2–2.5 metres tall, and powerfully built. Judging from witness drawings, there seems little doubt that the Beast is a werewolf.

THE **BEAST** OF BRAY ROAD
Tailing Wisconsin's Werewolf

Linda S. Godfrey

▲ The story of the Beast has inspired a book.

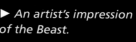

▶ An artist's impression of the Beast.

▲ *Most people agree that the Beast is almost certainly a werewolf.*

Danger to humans

The Beast has not yet attacked and killed a human, but there have been several near misses. A typical encounter happened when two men in a car spotted a large creature in the road. As they got closer they realised it was the Beast. As one of them rolled down the window for a better look, the Beast attacked. The men sped off – but the car was raked down the side by powerful claws.

What is the Beast?

There are several theories about what the Beast may be. The most popular is that it is a werewolf, and at least one witness claims to have seen the Beast transforming itself from wolf form. Among the other possibilities are three creatures from Native American **myths**:

- Shunka wara'kin – a mythical creature like a cross between a wolf and a hyena, which walks on its back legs.

- Amarok, a giant wolf-like creature that tracks and kills anyone foolish enough to hunt alone at night.

- A skinwalker (see pages 16–17).

21

Lobisomem of Brazil

If there's one place a werewolf hunter really needs to visit at least once, it's the Brazilian town of Joanópolis. There are more werewolf sightings in Joanópolis than anywhere else in the world.

In Brazil, werewolves are known as lobisomem. They are hideous wolf-like creatures, with razor-sharp teeth and red, glowing eyes. What they desire above all else is raw meat.

▲ *Turn a corner in the Brazilian city of Joanópolis late at night, and you might find a lobisomem lurking in your path...*

Werewolf Fact File

Name: Lobisomem
Location: Brazil
Age: not known

Behaviour and characteristics

Lobisomem change into wolves when they arrive at a crossroads at midnight on a Friday. Unlike many other werewolves, they do not need a full moon. Most werewolf hunters agree that lobisomem can only take human form again by finding the same crossroads, again at midnight.

Becoming a lobisomem

There are several ways of becoming a lobisomem:
• People say that the seventh child of the same sex born in a row will become a lobisomem.
• Others say that if the eighth child is a boy after seven girls, he will become a lobisomem.
• A lobisomem bite will transmit the werewolf curse.

Lobisomem are extremely hard to kill in wolf form, though they can be destroyed using silver weapons.

▲ *Lobisomem mainly feed on dead animals, but if they meet a human – they attack!*

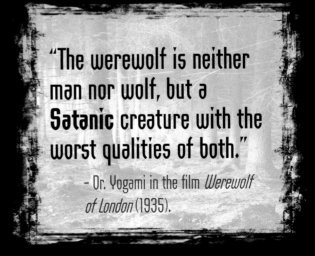

"The werewolf is neither man nor wolf, but a **Satanic** creature with the worst qualities of both."

– Dr. Yogami in the film *Werewolf of London* (1935).

The Benandanti werewolves

As a werewolf hunter, you become used to werewolves being enemies. But there is another category of werewolf: the ones who actually fight evil.

Werewolf Fact File

Name: Benandanti
Location: Originally Italy
Age: at least 600 years

▲ A band of Benandanti head into battle, as a Malandanti witch swoops down to attack them.

Guardians

These werewolves are known as the Benandanti. For hundreds of years they have guarded the paths from the Underworld to the world of the living. Their special enemies are the Malandanti, an evil group of witches.

24

Benandanti behaviour

By day, the Benandanti look human, but at night their true nature is revealed. They transform into supernatural, wolf-like creatures, to do battle with the forces of evil.

It is impossible to become a Benandanti by choice. You have to be born one. Membership does not run in families. Instead, it is a 'gift' given to only a few people in each **generation**.

▶ *The Benandanti look ferocious, but are in fact a force for good.*

Beware the false Benandanti

A careful werewolf hunter will be very wary of anyone claiming to be a Benandanti. Some time after about 1600 their sworn enemies, the witches, began to **infiltrate** the Benandanti ranks. The werewolves kept their identities hidden, and exist now only as a secret society. This means that anyone who openly claims to be a Benandanti is more likely to be a witch.

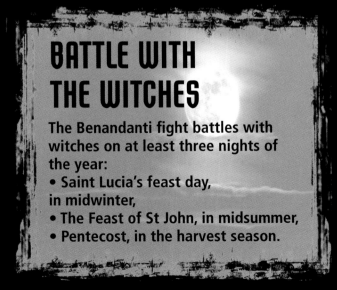

BATTLE WITH THE WITCHES

The Benandanti fight battles with witches on at least three nights of the year:
• Saint Lucia's feast day, in midwinter,
• The Feast of St John, in midsummer,
• Pentecost, in the harvest season.

Werewolves at the movies

Werewolves have always been popular villains in horror movies. Recently, some have tried to show werewolves in a positive, romantic light. Don't be fooled though! There are still plenty of bloodthirsty ones out there...

▲ Werewolves can be terrifying horror movie villains.

The Wolfman

The Wolfman (1941) was the film that kick-started the modern werewolf craze. It told the story of a man who is bitten when defending a woman from a werewolf. In the end, he becomes a werewolf himself, and has to be killed.

Twilight

The *Twilight* films centre on the relationship between Bella Swan and the vampire Edward Cullen. But one of the key characters in the films is the Native American Jacob Black, who is able to transform himself into a wolf. Jacob and other shape-shifting members of his tribe help to save Bella from her enemies on several occasions.

▼ Bella is drawn to the mysterious shape-shifter Jacob Black in the Twilight *films.*

Underworld

The Underworld series of movies features a world where vampires and a species of werewolves called Lycans are deadly rivals. The Lycans were created when a wolf bit an immortal child. Spanning hundreds of years, the movies are set in a bleak, cheerless land.

> "You really, honestly don't mind that I morph into a giant dog?"
>
> – Jacob Black to Bella Swan in *New Moon.*

Other man-beasts

As every werewolf hunter knows, werewolves aren't the only dangerous half-man, half-beasts you have to watch out for. Often a report of a werewolf turns out to be something else. These are just a few of the other monsters that crop up from time to time.

"Those things out there are REAL. If they're real, what else is real? You know what lives in the shadows now. You may never get another night's sleep as long as you live."

– Megan, in the movie *The Dog Soldiers* (2002)

The Goatman

First sighted: 1957
Location: mainly Maryland, but as far south as Texas and as far north as Canada
With the legs of a goat, a man's upper body, and a horned head, the Goatman certainly isn't hard to spot. He has attacked several people, and is said to have killed many pets. His victims are often couples who have parked their car in **secluded** places.

An artist's impression of the Goatman, who has been terrifying people in the USA and Canada for over 50 years.

Momo

First sighted: July 1971
Location: Missouri, USA
Momo is short for 'Missouri Monster'. Standing 2.2 metres tall, and covered in thick, black fur, Momo is said to smell worse than week-old rubbish. It is regularly reported to have eaten people's dogs, but has not yet attacked humans.

◀ *It's hard to be sure what's more unpleasant about Momo – the way he looks, or the terrible way he smells!*

The Monkey Man

First sighted: 2001
Location: New Delhi, India
The Monkey Man is about 1.2 metres tall, but is very strong and agile. He has attacked several people in New Delhi, India since 2001. Monkey Man has bitten and scratched people throughout the city, and is said to have caused at least two deaths as people fled from him in a panic.

▲ *Could this be India's mysterious Monkey Man?*

Technical information

Words from this book:

bestial
beast-like and disgusting

consequences
outcomes or results

curse
harm that is caused to someone by a
supernatural power

generation
people born at around the same time

immune
unable to be harmed by something

incantation
spell or charm

infiltrate
become part of a group

insatiable
impossible to satisfy

kindred
members of the same family

Lent
forty days leading up to Easter, when
some Christians follow various rules
about what they can eat and how they
should behave

lynched
illegally killed

myth
ancient story

Satanic
extremely evil

secluded
lonely or isolated

shape-shifting
able to change form,
for example from a
human into
a wolf

trait
a feature or quality of something

transformed
changed into a different form

wracked
full of pain

Equipment

Never skimp on your werewolf-hunting
equipment: it is always worth spending
the maximum possible on it. After all,
one day your life might depend on it!

Silver weapons
Always check if there is a hallmark (a
mark stamped into a real silver) to make
sure they really are silver. You don't want
to discover just as a werewolf closes in
that they're only PART silver, and don't
work.

Used bullets tend not to be available,
but other secondhand weapons will be
fine. Never buy secondhand unless you
can meet the previous owner – though
if they're dead, it might be a sign that
the weapons don't work all that well.

Herbs, potions, etc.
Always buy these as fresh as possible.

Ideally, get your supplies in the area
where the werewolf you are hunting
lives. That way everything will be
suited to fighting the local werewolf
population.

More werewolf information

Other books

A Practical Guide To Vampires Werewolves and Other Shapeshifters Anita Ganeri (Wayland, 2010)
Contains basic information about werewolves and other shape-shifting monsters from around the world.

Tales Of Horror: Werewolves Jim Pipe (ticktock Media, 2006)
A great collection of rollicking werewolf stories, guaranteed to have you hiding under the covers at night!

Wolf Man Susan Gates (Usborne Publishing, 2009)
A roller-coaster ride of an adventure story, this book is a mystery with a strange, supernatural twist.

Although the following are adult titles, they would be useful to confident readers who want to find out more:
Werewolves: A Field Guide to Shapeshifters, Lycanthropes and Man-Beasts Bob Curran (New Page Books, 2009)
The Werewolf Book: The Encyclopaedia of Shape-Shifting Beings Brad Steiger (Gale Publishing, 1999)

The Internet

www.monstropedia.org
This is a great, big rambling site, which is absolutely full of information about all kinds of weird, supernatural and scary creatures. To get to the werewolves section, click on 'Shapeshifters', then 'Werewolves'.

www.werewolves.com
All kinds of information is found on this site: tips about forthcoming werewolf movies; tales of werewolves from hundreds of years ago; or jokey articles about Things You Could Get Away With If You Were A Werewolf ("Always win the prize for Best Costume at Halloween parties"...).

Movies and DVDs

Check the werewolves.com website at http://www.werewolves.com/werewolf-movies-to-watch-out-for/ for forthcoming werewolf movies. Here are some classics, both old and new:

The Wolfman (1941, dir. George Waggner)
The all-time classic werewolf movie. The script was influenced by writer Curt Siodmak's experiences in Nazi Germany before World War II.

The Howling (1981, dir. Joe Dante)
From the same director as *Gremlins*, this is a much darker, scarier movie. A reporter and her husband decide to take a holiday in a lonely village. There's just one problem: it's home to a community of werewolves.

Dog Soldiers (2002, dir. Neil Marshall)
A group of soldiers out on patrol in the wilds of Scotland find themselves under attack by a family of werewolves. They take shelter in a lonely farmhouse – but all is not what it seems... Will any of them survive the night?

Index

First published in 2012 by
Franklin Watts
338 Euston Road
London NW1 3BH

Franklin Watts Australia
Level 17/207 Kent Street
Sydney NSW 2000

Copyright © Franklin Watts 2011

All rights reserved.

Series editors: Adrian Cole and Julia Bird
Art director: Jonathan Hair
Design: Mayer Media
Picture research: Diana Morris

ISBN 978 1 4451 0121 7

Dewey number: 398.4'69

A CIP catalogue record for this book
is available from the British Library.

Printed in China

Franklin Watts is a division of
Hachette Children's Books,
an Hachette UK company.
www.hachette.co.uk

Acknowledgements:
Alhovik/Shutterstock: 4-5 b/g. Arfey/Shutterstock: 20br.
The Art Archive/Alamy: 24b. Marilyn Barbone/Shutterstock:
30bl, 5brt. Stephane Bidouze/Shutterstock: 11b.
www.bigearthpublishing.com. Artwork by Jeff Easley: 20bl.
Blueberg/Alamy: 22t. © 2010 The British Library, London: 5t.
Jackie Carvey/Shutterstock: 2c. Hal D Crawford from" The
Aliens", 1970, Crawford, Hayden Hewes and Kietha Hewes:
29tl. Sergei Devyatkin/Shutterstock: 5br, 30tr.
DLILLC/Corbis: 12bl. Terrance Emerson/Shutterstock: 19t.
Everett Collection/Rex Features: 4t. Fabio Fersa/Shutterstock:
4bl. Fortean PL/Topfoto: 9t. The Granger Collection/
Topfoto: 15bl. Eric Isselée/Shutterstock: 18b. Amy Johansson/
Shutterstock: 11tl, 23b, 27c. jumping sack/Shutterstock: 13r.
Kojot/Shutterstock: 6b, 7c, 13bl, 15br, 17tr, 19b, 25b, 28tr.
© Lions Gate/Everett Collection/Rex Features: 16b.
© Lee Luker: 28b. Natalia Lukiyanova/frenta/Shutterstock:
3tr, 8t, 10t, 12c, 14t, 16tr, 18c, 20tr, 22b, 24c. Ing. Schieder
Markus/Shutterstock: 8b. Moviestore Collection Ltd/Alamy:
27b. Nyord/Shutterstock: 23t. Photos12/Alamy: 21, 26.
Picturepartners/Shutterstock: 5bl. Jean-Pierre Pieuchot/
Getty Images: 14b. Scott Rothstein/Shutterstock: 4bc, 12tl,
16tl, 20tl, 24tl, 28tl. Roberto A Sanchez/istockphoto: 29br.
Elzbieta Sekowska /Shutterstock: 17tc. Porojinicu Stellan/
Shutterstock: 10b. Tom Tietz/istockphoto: 17b.
Trent/Fotolia: front cover. Universal/Everett Collection/Rex
Features: 7t. www.vafis.info: 11t. Anthony Wallis/Fortean PL/
Topfoto: 25t. Igor Xill/Shutterstock: 6c.

Every attempt has been made to clear copyright.
Should there be any inadvertent omission please
apply to the publisher for rectification.